Stupid Poems 15

Stupid Poems 15

Ian Vannoey

Copyright © 2020 Ian Vannoey

The moral right of the author has been asserted.
Apart from any fair dealing for the purposes of research or private study, or criticism or review, as permitted under the Copyright, Designs and Patents Act 1988, this publication may only be reproduced, stored or transmitted, in any form or by any means, with the prior permission in writing of the publishers, or in the case of reprographic reproduction in accordance with the terms of licences issued by the Copyright Licensing Agency. Enquiries concerning reproduction outside those terms should be sent to the publishers.

Matador
9 Priory Business Park,
Wistow Road, Kibworth Beauchamp,
Leicestershire. LE8 0RX
Tel: 0116 279 2299

Email: books@troubador.co.uk
Web: www.troubador.co.uk/matador
Twitter: @matadorbooks

ISBN 978 1838592 783

British Library Cataloguing in Publication Data.
A catalogue record for this book is available from the British Library.

Typeset by Troubador Publishing Ltd, Leicester, UK

Matador is an imprint of Troubador Publishing Ltd

Contents

Speipnir	1
Incitatus	2
Things Donald Trump is unlikely to say	3
Why did ... cross the road jokes	4
A flamingo's lament	6
Sloping water	8
Alternative names for WD40	9
Why it's not a good idea to use a hedgehog as a bath sponge	10
Things with stripes	11
The bees' knees	12
The names of buildings	13
A visit to Earth by super-intelligent aliens	14
Am I the only person in the world who is not interested in football?	15
I'm so worried about getting my umbrella wet	16
Putting lipstick on a pig	17
The beard tax	18
There is no catflap at no. 10	19
Does a cat know it's a cat?	20
The Irish backstop	21
Ode to underpants	23
Lady Macbeth's first name	24
The world is flat	25

Meeting of the Red-Crested Pochard Association of Moldova	26
The Vikings did not wear horned helmets	27
I've just bought a giraffe but can't get it home	28
William Shakespeare's lesser-known brother Gareth	29
The Brexit chat-up	30
Poem in which the last word in every line is the same as the first word	31
Silly poem about the Israeli Prime Minister, Yogi Bear, babies and sheep	32
Why it's a good idea to cry over spilt milk	33
Poem in celebration of the birth of Archie Harrison Mountbatten-Windsor	34
Medea	36
To be US President it helps to have a strange name	37
Conservative leadership candidate anagrams	38
The district nurse came to take a blood sample from me but I persuaded her to take it from my cat instead	40
The Odyssey	41
Fork lift truck	42
Painting the town red	43
You need ears to keep your glasses on	44
Is there a word that rhymes with 'purple'?	45
The song of the insurance salesman	46
If we kept kangaroos instead of dogs...	47

Sleipnir

(In Norse mythology the god Odin had a horse, called Sleipnir, with eight legs.)

You would expect that, being a god,
Odin's horse is rather odd.
It doesn't fly, or lay eggs.
Odin's horse has eight legs.
Having eight legs is super, though,
The miles per horseshoe ratio is low.
I bet you never thought to ride a
Horse that's somewhat like a spider.
He doesn't care about going lame:
With all those spares it's all the same.
Being a horse is really great
If your number of legs is eight.

Incitatus

(This another poem about a horse. The Roman emperor Caligula, who was completely mad, had a horse, called Incitatus, of which he was so fond he tried to make it his fellow consul; the second most important individual in the empire.)

He should have the ability
To bring the state stability.
The new consul's able
To make the state a stable.
As a politician,
He's better than a human.
He eats far more hay
Than Theresa May.
At jumping a hurdle,
Better than Churchill.
You'll never see Napoleon
Caught with a saddle on.
Herbert Asquith
Never went to the blacksmith.
To share power I need
To have my trusty steed.

Things Donald Trump is unlikely to say

'Let's objectively weigh up all the evidence.'
'coherent foreign policy'
'I respectfully disagree.'
'I'm so grateful to the media for giving me so much publicity.'
'Everybody is entitled to be treated with respect.'
'I went to Britain and was greeted by huge cheering crowds.'*
'The US constitution is designed to limit the power of the president.'
'The USA is a nation built on immigration.'
'With all due modesty,…'
'Not the biggest/best/worst ever, but quite big/good/bad.'
'A leader should try to unite the people.'
'Guns are dangerous.'
'A president should have at least a basic knowledge of history, geography, economics, and science.'
'At least I'm consistent.'
'What's Twitter?'
'You can disagree with someone without insulting them'.
'Evidence-based policy'.
'Sorry'

*Actually, he has said this now. I naively thought that even he wouldn't lie so outrageously.

Why did ... cross the road jokes

Why did the zebra cross the road?
To use the zebra crossing.

Why did the bee cross the road?
It was a B road.

Why did the miner cross the road?
It was a minor road.

Why did the major cross the road?
Too obvious.

Why did the pantomime villain cross the road?
Oh no he didn't.

Why did the boomerang cross the road?
It was on the other side to start with.

Why did the Vikings cross the road?
To loot and pillage the other side.

Why did Julius Caesar cross the road?
It caused less trouble than crossing the Rubicon.

Why did Christopher Columbus cross the road?
It was less far to go than crossing the Atlantic.

Why did Lenin cross the road?
To get to a lamp-post he could climb on and sing 'I'm Lenin on a lamp-post…'

Why did Donald Trump cross the road?
He didn't - this is fake news.

A flamingo's lament

You might think
Being pink
Is quite pretty,
But it's shitty
Standing here
Till fish appear.
I'm so jealous
Of warm wellies
Which you oughtta
Wear in water.
P'raps one day
I'll soar away;
I'd swoop and glide,
On air currents ride.
I'd spot my prey
From far away,
Way up high,
In the sky.
I'd dive through space
With speed and grace.
I'd be spectacular,
And David Attenborough
Would see me,
And bring TV.

I'd be a creature
Who would feature
On the telly.
I'd need no welly,
But this dream's fading;
I'm stuck with wading.

Sloping water

All my life I've been hoping
To find a water surface sloping.
A water surface that's not level
Is not bad, it isn't evil.
Think what fun it would be
If you could downhill water ski.
I could never get my fill
Of sailing up and down a hill.
Ferry fares may go up
Every time they're sailing up.
Going to a downhill coast,
Turn off the engines and just coast.
If your garden steeply slopes
You might even nurture hopes
Of putting in a fish pond,
If of this idea you're fond.
It would not be very silly
To talk of sea being hilly.
A boring transatlantic cruise
Could then offer lovely views.
So this is why we all oughtta
Look around for sloping water.

Alternative names for WD40

WD40 is useful if
Locks and hinges are too stiff,
But have you ever had the thought:
If it were not called WD fort-
Y but XP28,
Would it be just as great?
Could EQ73
Be also used for getting things free?
Could you fix a squeaky door
By squirting LM34?
Is there anything you could fix
By using NA86?
Would a can of CT9
Be as useful or as fine?
Would WD40 be the same
If it had a different name?

Why it's not a good idea to use a hedgehog as a bath sponge

When you have a bath you oughtta
Use a sponge with soap and water.
If a hedgehog sponge you pick
You'll feel something of a prick.
With a hedgehog sponge the catch is
You'll be left with lots of scratches.
When you use it you'll say "Crikey!
This hedgehog's skin is all spiky!"
In one respect it's really fine:
It's better than a porcupine.
You want a sponge that's soft and gentle.
If you don't you must be mental.
A hedgehog sponge will make you shout.
So let the hedgehogs run about.

Things with stripes

Zebras and tigers,
Deck-chairs and pyjamas,
Football shirts, prison shirts,
All kinds of stripy shirts,
Blazers on old cricket players,
Cake that comes in coloured layers,
None of these are nicer than
Ice-cream Neapolitan.
Wouldn't it be quaint
To get stripy paint?

IAN VANNOEY

The bees' knees

If it's true that bees have knees they must be very small.
Personally I rather doubt that bees have knees at all.
Just the thought that bees have knees, I find rather funny.
Although, perhaps, they need knees in order to make honey.
It could be that they need knees when they make each lot.
They have to kneel on the floor to stir their honey pot.
Mums and dads tell baby bees, when they're in the hive:
"If you wish to beelong, then you must beehave."
If it's true that bees have knees, they might have toes and feet;
Find out on the Internet by going to Buzzfeet.
This poem now is ending, but I think I will fail
To think of a good ending: a sting in the tail.

The names of buildings

(Some buildings have nicknames because of objects they resemble. Examples are the Gherkin and the Shard in London, the Cheesegrater (the Leadenhall Building, also in London), and the Wedding Cake (the NLA Tower in Croydon). Here are some more suggestions.)

I don't suppose you'll ever see
A building called the Lavatory.
What is more I do not think
You'd ever be inside the Sink.
Nobody would ever rush
To work inside the Toilet Brush.
It may be that you'd be much keener
To work inside the Vacuum Cleaner.
If you find this thought appealing,
The Hoover Building is in Ealing.

(true)

A visit to Earth by super-intelligent aliens

From light-years away
The aliens came to say:
"People of Earth,
We've watched Earth since its birth.
Since we appeared,
We must seem rather weird.
You've seen nothing stranger,
But your planet's now in danger.
We've come to rescue you.
Who will speak for you?"
So the people all go "Err…"
So the aliens prefer
To quickly disappear.
"There's no intelligence here."

Am I the only person in the world who is not interested in football?

I don't come from another planet,
When hungry, I don't snack on granite.
The number of heads I have is one.
I don't count blades of grass for fun.
I'm not sexually attracted to my cat.
I'm not at all weird like that.
However, I'm a most odd chap.
I don't care about the World Cup.

I'm so worried about getting my umbrella wet

Whenever it is in the rain,
My umbrella just gets wet again.
I just wish it would not get
Rained upon and soaking wet.
What I want (I don't know why)
Is that it always stays quite dry.
And so, if you can believe it,
Back at home is where I leave it.
When it rains, when I am walking,
I prefer to get a soaking.
Though it seems the height of folly,
At least I'll have a nice dry brolly.

Putting lipstick on a pig

Should you ever take up
The practice of pig make-up,
Find a pig that will
Conveniently keep still.
You'll quickly find out
Its lips below its snout.
You'll soon have your piggy
Looking really pretty.
A touch of eye liner
Will make it look still finer.
You can choose a blusher
That suits its natural colour.
You will have a porker
That really is a corker.

The beard tax

(As part of his campaign to make Russia more modern and European, Tsar Peter the Great levied a tax on beards).

Russia's a tax haven
If you are clean shaven.
If you've a beard the fact is
You will have higher taxes.
If your beard is heavy,
You'll have a greater levy.
Even a goatee
Incurs a modest fee.
You might think this unfair,
If you have facial hair.
If a beard you've got,
It will cost you a lot.

There is no catflap at no.10

(The front door of no.10 Downing Street has no catflap. This means that the Downing Street cat (Larry) has to wait for someone to open the door.)

If you think Brexit's difficult then
Try exiting no.10.
It really isn't very great
That by the door I have to wait
Till someone opens up the door.
I cannot open it with my paw.
I cannot go through a catflap.
I have to wait and take a catnap.
I have to say this is a shabby
Way in which to treat a tabby.
I cannot just go out and gad about.
It's not something I'm in a flap about.
British Government should be streamline,
So that it can suit a feline.
If I could then I would choose
To raise this point at PMQs.
I really find it rather sinister
That the house of our Prime Minister
Is so very, very shitty
That it's not right for a kitty.

IAN VANNOEY

Does a cat know it's a cat?

(There was a song called *Remember You're a Womble*. This suggests that a womble knows that it's a womble, although it may forget. Do other animals know what species they are?)

Do you think a cat
Knows it's not a rat?
Is it well aware
That it's not a bear?
Does it say "Of course,
I am not a horse"?
Does it ever think
That it is a mink?
Is it in the habit
Of thinking it's a rabbit?
Does it ever wake
Thinking it's a snake?
Does it ever wish
That it were a fish?
If it were to try it,
It would change its diet.
It would have to get
Used to being wet.
Does a polar bear
Know it's not a hare?
Is an animal's kind
On an animal's mind?

The Irish Backstop

(If you've been following the Brexit news, you will know about this; you might even understand it.)

Britain's leaving the EU,
But what does an Irish backstop do?
Perhaps it's a post stuck in the ground.
Throughout Ireland they are found,
At the end of each cul-de-sac
To stop you driving too far back.
Opposite an Irish backstop
You might find an Irish frontstop.
If you ever drive in Eire,
Of the backstops do take care.
Of the backstops do be wary
In Dublin, Cork or Dun Laoghaire*.
P'raps it's a cricket fielding position.
If you field there you'll be wishin'
That the ball flies to you.
Catch the ball is what you'd do.
You will find the Irish backstop
T'ween short fine backstop and deep square backstop.
Or perhaps an Irish backstop
Is a special kind of doorstop.
Maybe this is what it's for:

IAN VANNOEY

On the floor beside the door
A heavy weight upon the mat
Stops the door from slamming shut,
So you can make a rapid exit,
Or p'raps it is to do with Brexit.

*this rhymes (honestly)

Ode to underpants

They're usually made of cotton,
And cover up your bottom,
And so it is, it seems,
They're underneath your jeans.
There are just two sorts:
Briefs and boxer shorts.
If they are good fits,
They'll cover up your bits.
Often they are white,
But, perhaps, they might
Be a different hue;
Maybe black or blue.
Something's quite fantastic:
The waistband is elastic.
So let us all give thanks
That we have underpants.

Lady Macbeth's first name

When she married she took the name
Of her husband, which was the same.
What was she called as a rule
In the time she was at school?
She was, perhaps, Elizabeth,
And so her name was Beth Macbeth.
Elizabeth Macbeth, her full name that is,
Or perhaps she was called Gladys,
Or perhaps she was called Tracy,
Or perhaps she was called Stacey.
She might be Susan, known as Sue,
So Sue Macbeth would have to do.
I think it would be really great
If, perchance, her name were Kate.
Or, perhaps, she was the bearer
Of the Christian name of Sarah.
Shakespeare was the immortal bard,
But thinking of names he found quite hard.

The world is flat

(Some people in the USA believe the world is flat. For 'proof' that the world is not round, go to https://www.youtube.com/watch?v=-Ax_YpQsy88)

Throw out your atlases and your maps.
They are all wrong; the world is flat.
You are really just a fool,
If you believed the stuff at school.
It is just a silly tale
That you can round-the-world sail.
Magellan, Drake and all those guys
Were telling just a lot of lies.
Pictures from space that they make:
Don't believe them; they're all fake.
Greeks and arabs who measured the Earth
Did not do anything of worth.
Don't believe those who've found
Solid evidence the world is round.

Meeting of the Red-Crested Pochard Association of Moldova

(the red-crested pochard is a species of duck which is rare in Moldova, where there are just 70-100 breeding pairs).

It is hard
For the pochard,
And you might think
We'll be extinct,
And it's over
In Moldova.
But we're a duck
Who has luck.
Have no fear,
You will hear
Pochards quacking;
We won't be lacking,
In this land
We'll take a stand.
We'll be here
For many a year.

The Vikings did not wear horned helmets

(It is widely believed that the Vikings wore helmets with horns, but this is a myth).

You cannot go into battle
Looking like a herd of cattle.
Just because I am a Viking
Does not mean I have a liking
For having horns on my hat.
One disadvantage is that,
If you have a hat with horns,
It will get caught up in the thorns.
It's not that it has got no point.
To tell the truth it's got two points.
There are times I feel quite horny;
This doesn't mean my hat is horny.
You cannot go and pillage and loot
When people say "Your hat's a hoot!"
The truth is I have never worn
A helmet with a single horn.

IAN VANNOEY

I've just bought a giraffe but can't get it home

A new giraffe I have just bought.
'What a cool idea' I thought.
But then I thought 'How the heck
Do I cope with this long neck?'
Where I live is rather far.
I cannot get it in the car.
I tried to take it on the bus.
The driver made quite a fuss.
It was the same on the train.
Getting a ticket was a pain.
And so we are out of luck.
My giraffe and I are stuck.
I cannot leave it running wild
To frighten any passing child.
Actually he quite likes it here;
We could be here for many a year.
He eats the leaves from off the trees.
The local council won't be pleased.
All the leaves he finds quite yummy.
And with lamp posts he is chummy.
But I just want my nice warm bed.
We must slowly homeward tread.
On reflection it was daft
To lash out on a new giraffe.

William Shakespeare's lesser-known brother Gareth

William Shakespeare's brother's name is
Gareth, who is not so famous.
Gareth Shakespeare didn't write stuff.
One playwright in the family was enough.
Unlike his brother, he didn't spend days
Writing sonnets and writing plays.
So what did Gareth do, actually?
Did he work on a farm, or in a factory?
Was he a plumber, a dentist or a miller?
A bus-driver or a serial killer?
I'm afraid that this is a mystery.
Gareth has been written out of history.
Among the famous he's not listed.
But I am sure that he existed.
When William created Romeo,
He said "What do you think of this, bro?"
Gareth said "Let him get
A girl-friend; call her Juliet."
Millions of people have, since then, read it.
But poor old Gareth gets no credit.

The Brexit chat-up

Come back to my place; it is roomy and
We can form a customs union.
We will have such a lark; it
Seems we make a single market.
My backstop you'll not want to exit,
When you've seen my hard Brexit.
You'll see that I am really nifty
As I revoke my Article 50.
I'm not just sowing wild oats.
I like lots of meaningful votes.
So come with me; you won't regret it.
It will get our minds off Brexit.

Poem in which the last word in every line is the same as the first word

Hannibal crossed the Alps, did Hannibal.
Cannibals get eaten by cannibals.
Light that's not heavy is light.
Tights too small are tight.
Stabled horses are stable.
Table an amendment at the table.
Wear out the clothes you wear.
Fair are the folk at the fair.
Drum up support on a drum.
Hum so you make a hum.
May was Prime Minister last May.
May not be Prime Minister this May.

IAN VANNOEY

Silly poem about the Israeli Prime Minister, Yogi Bear, babies, and sheep

Benjamin Netanyahu is Bibi.
Bebé is Spanish for baby.
Bibi is Netanyahu.
Yogi's sidekick was Boo Boo.
Sheep and lambs go baa baa.
These poems get silliar and silliar.

Why it's a good idea to cry over spilt milk

You'll find your whole world crashing
If a little milk you're splashing.
If it's all spilt on the floor,
You really can't take any more.
You will be overcome by grief,
And so it is a great relief
If you should let out a cry,
And so surely this is why,
If you spill your milk or cream,
It does you good to shout and scream.
It really is a silly notion
That you shouldn't show emotion.
And it really does not follow
That you should suppress your sorrow.

IAN VANNOEY

Poem in celebration of the birth of Archie Harrison Mountbatten-Windsor

(I'm still hoping to be poet laureate)

Do you think Harry's happy
To change a royal nappy?
Or, perhaps, a royal
Baby has a loyal
Servant who says "Maybe,
It's time to change the baby".
A servant of this type has
To change the royal diapers.
Has the little boy
A special furry toy?
Perhaps Meghan says "Aw gee,
Let's get a furry corgi".
Will the parents rave
About the first royal wave?
They will have such fun
If his first word is 'one'.
They'll say "It's uncanny,
He's just like his great granny".
You have to applaud
The names he has been called.
His first name is Archie,

And that's not stiff and starchy.
His second name is Harrison;
A good name for Harry's son.

Medea

This tale from ancient Greece turned out to be one of these
That was put on the stage in a play by Euripides.
She's a fierce and scary character, and Medea's story
Has an ending that's tragic, brutal, and gory.
Jason and the Argonauts sail forth from Greece
Across the Black Sea to Colchis, to get the Golden Fleece.
Medea is a princess, in that savage land.
She falls in love with Jason, when he arrives with his band.
She uses magic arts, as she is a sorceress,
And gives aid to Jason to help him in his quest.
She bears him two children, and everything is swell.
From then on things do not go so well.
When they back to Greece her situation's lousy,
As Jason rejects her so he can marry Glauce.
Medea is livid; you really should have heard 'er.
She puts paid to Glauce; that's not her only murder.
You might think she's an affectionate, kind and loving mummy,
But, to spite Jason, she stabs her children in the tummy.
Try to think of anything that's horrible and nasty,
Greek tragedy, you can be sure, had something far more ghastly.

To be US President it helps to have a strange Christian name

To be President of the USA,
It really helps if you can say:
"My name is odd too like these:
Lyndon, Barrack and Ulysses".
But will it be the same story
Next year, for Beto, Kamala or Cory?

Conservative leadership candidate anagrams

Boris Johnson
Boss iron John

Michael Gove
Ha! Glove mice

Jeremy Hunt
Jury me then

Andrea Leadsom
A real sand dome

Dominic Raab
I'm in a cod bar

Matt Hancock
Mock at chant

Rory Stewart
Err Tory swat

Esther Mcvey
Cheer my vest

STUPID POEMS 15

James Cleverly
Rev cell jam. Yes!

Sajid Javid
You try thinking of a phrase of ten letters with two Js!

Then there's the Speaker:

John Bercow
Hen crow job

Meanwhile in Europe:

Jean-Claude Juncker
June raced lace junk

Donald Tusk
Not dusk lad

Michel Barnier
He crab rim line

Guy Verhofstadt
Farty vest dough

(maybe I should get out more)

The district nurse came to take a blood sample from me but I persuaded her to take it from my cat instead

Your sample we have analysed,
And you will be quite surprised.
Prepare yourself for nasty news.
It's not the outcome you would choose.
We had to check your species too and
We have found you are not human.
It's not your health; this will be fine.
It's simply that you are a feline.
Have you had a tail or fur?
Do you ever miaow or purr?
The best advice that you can get:
Go and register with a vet.

The Odyssey

Odysseus spent ten years laying siege to Troy,
And ten years coming home; what a clever boy!

Fork lift truck

If you drop a spoon,
You'll pick it up quite soon.
If a knife goes on the deck,
You'll just say "What the heck".
However, let us talk
Of when you drop a fork.
You'll be out of luck.
You'll need a fork lift truck.
A special kind of truck, you see,
Lifts this piece of cutlery.
To raise a fork up higher,
A truck you'll have to hire.
So, when you lay the table,
Have a truck available.

Painting the town red

An all-red town might seem quaint,
But you would need a lot of paint.
Although it may have lots of plusses,
You would need a lot of brushes.
What would make you really sad is
You'd never find enough ladders.
A colour scheme without variety
Would only cause much anxiety.
Red traffic lights cannot say 'go',
So the traffic would not flow.
Pedestrian crossings would be lost;
You would not know where to cross.
Red-painted windows would be stopping
Any chance of window shopping.
One other thing would come with it:
The whole town is a red-light district.

IAN VANNOEY

You need ears to keep your glasses on

On the side of your head,
It can be said,
There is an ear,
Which doesn't just hear.
Its major task is
To keep on your glasses.
So have no fears:
As we have ears,
Your specs stay in place
On the front of your face.
Without doing this job,
We'd have a prob.
I s'pose specs could hang,
Using some string,
Down from your hair,
But that's not secure.
Instead of spectacles
We could have two monocles,
But can you imagine
If this were the fashion?
So let's give three cheers
That we have ears.

Is there a word that rhymes with 'purple'?

A very attractive colour is purple.
There was a film called The Colour Purple.
But I can't think of a word that rhymes with 'purple'.
Here are some words that could rhyme with purple.
Excuse me, I must go for a gurple.
If I were a sparrow, I'd love to chirple.
If you don't mind, I'm about to burple.
Cover your ears, for I feel like a wurple.
If it feels sore, then pour on some turple.
I can put up with most things, but please don't lurple.
You have to be strong to join in the grurple.
Excuse me, could I borrow your thirple?
If these were words they'd rhyme with purple.

I've investigated this on the Internet. According to one website, purple has no English rhyme, along with orange, silver, month, ninth, wolf, opus, dangerous, marathon and discombobulate. However, another website offers curple (the rump of a horse), hirple (walk with a limp) and nurple (slang for roughly twisting a nipple).

IAN VANNOEY

The song of the insurance salesmen

We are the lads who are hearty and jolly, see,
And we'll sell you an insurance policy.
We'll march across the country, far and wide.
We'll insure your house and everything inside.
The insurance man laughs; the insurance man sings.
We'll insure your car, your life and your things.
We'll insure anything, however small or big.
We'll insure your legs, your parrot or your wig.
If you see us coming in our suits and our ties,
You'll go the other way, if you are wise.
And if, by chance, we catch you, by some mishap,
We'll spout a load of flannel; we'll talk a load of crap.
If you think our policy is rather expensive,
It's because its coverage is so extensive.
This is a job in which it's really fun to be:
A salesman for an insurance company.

If we kept kangaroos instead of dogs…

From the great Australian outback,
You could have one out the back.
But would you know what to do,
If you had a kangaroo?
Every day you'd have to stop,
And take it out for a hop.
You would see signs which read:
'Your kangaroo must have a lead.'
Lots of folks would love to go
To Cruft's kangaroo show.
Fox hunts would always choose
To have a pack of kangaroos.
Animals with a pouch in front
Would always help them with their hunt.
Guard kangaroos and guide kangaroos,
Police kangaroos and sniffer kangaroos,
Would help us in our daily jobs,
But would they be as good as dogs?

Lightning Source UK Ltd.
Milton Keynes UK
UKHW022210211119
353974UK00009B/560/P